POEMS

for Roy
with best wishes

David .

David Pownall

POEMS

Oberon Books
London

First published in this anthology by Oberon Books Ltd
521 Caledonian Road, London N7 9RH
020 7607 3637 / 020 7607 3629
info@oberonbooks.com / www.oberonbooks.com

A catalogue record for this book is available from the British Library.
Back cover photograph by Alex Pownall

ISBN: 1 84002 819 X / 978-1-84002-819-5

Printed in Great Britain by Antony Rowe Ltd, Chippenham.

Onvs whvth awel fe terfyn amser
(*Unless the wind blows time will stop*)

inscription – Vale of Usk

*For my sons
and the love of my life*

Poems

By the Serpentine

In the centre of that goose's brain
sits a speck of iron, magnetized –
an in-built compass by which
the creature navigates great journeys
to find its food, and breed.

Wild geese know where they're going –
tame ones only their patch.
A wild goose has metal in the head;
a tame one Christmas on the cards.
We sit here, hand in hand.

To a highflyer destination is all;
to the earthbound every move,
every mouthful, is suspect. Thought
is an annual feeling for migrants.
We sit here, kissing and kissing.

Observing us from the surface
of the lake, compasses idling, geese
advise what must happen in our lives –
lovers must find iron in the blood
to exchange winter for summer.

Imagine the Day

Born when frost grips hard – crying
somewhere in the chill darkness –
you arrived, sliding on ice into the world
without a word to me.

I was probably asleep, or playing somewhere,
being a nuisance to my mother, like you were
to yours, only more so – the pains of birth
being what they are.

Given what's happened between us, I would
have expected some sign for me to follow –
at least a message in code to be relayed:
follow the arrows and symbols.

But the Fates kept quiet, and the phone
we didn't have didn't ring. Yet in the silence
were notes of your coming. In the whirling void
was room for your arrival.

In my boy's heart I must have known.
I must have known you were here, hiding.
I told no one except the day itself, undertaking
to track you down and be your light's shadow.

Aubade for Alex

To make return to a time
before knowing you is to move
sideways, not backwards –
sideways from memory into fear
of the past. Without you
I'd be in shadowed country,
childhood and excitement
embedded in history's patterns,
transformed into shells.

A starry light still comes –
your closeness to that light
serves both of us. Without it,
without loving the child in the woman,
and you holding on to the child you know
in myself, I would be lost in the clay
of heavy country, forced to trudge
down furrows of clinging mire.

Recalling a prior existence
in which you're absent gets harder.
It's easier to imagine
the time before I was born,
or the extinctive days after leaving
this world. Held in your arms
as a freed dream, I am only
where you are, sharing the luck,
the dust, this morning light.

Where You Lived

In this city where you lived without me,
without even knowing I was alive,
there are empty chairs on balconies,
pillows undented on beds, rooms
where I am, but was not and you were.

A ghost precedes me down pavements
with your loved stride. I sit alone
at a crowded table, eating dishes
you would have ordered. Your recollections
of life here separate us. Mine are a void

being filled – yours, a breeze on a black sail
of ten years I was never in your eyes.
It will take many days to understand this city.
The knowledge I carry away will be light
but dangerous – your absence and presence in one.

Sydney, 1984

Flying with Birds of Paradise

Many exotic items evade the net thrown by a man's life –
some too small and turbulent to be held in the small mesh of meaning;
others so complex and wonderful we can hardly believe we share
being with them in this world.

When we drown it is not the past that flashes before our eyes –
that is a myth put about by ex-partners –
what happens is we see what we have never seen.
This glimpse into the depth of loss has nothing to do with eternal life.
It is merely a reminder of those things we missed
by being too proud to read in-flight magazines
when fearing death by aviation.

Today, seven miles above the earth,
sitting next to a novice pilot homewardbound to Jakarta
after training on our British simulators,
(we're so good at it, he says),
I discover my companion will not have a single real practice flight
before taking to the air with a full pay-load of human life.

He should not have told me this.
Suddenly our plane has a glass bottom. Smiling, he tries to reassure me,
mentioning co-pilotry. But if the hand upon the joystick is
used to a dream only…what then? I close the conversation down –
take refuge in an article penned
for the in-flight magazine about birds of paradise:
beautiful things that have so far survived the cruelties of progress –
which somehow includes my life.

From the glossy pages in my lap arises *The Enamelled Bird*,
a phoenix from the flames of my fear, sent to save me.
This bird is tiny, virtually weightless,
and rightly called marvellous.
Two long streamer-like feathers come out of the back of its head.

Without these stabilisers, it would fall over.
Apart from this (I quote the text) *it has no other claim to remarkability.*
What is remarkable is that as a species, mankind (including pilots)
has been forever falling over
and *The Enamelled Bird* hasn't.

A bird of paradise exists purely in order to perpetuate
its own idea of beauty – which, by some freak of evolution,
is also ours.
This is passing strange: rhinoceroses think each other beautiful –
we don't share that.
Unlike the sparrow the bird of paradise has no humbler meaning.
Even if starving to death, it would never come near your garden feeder
because the background would set it off
to disadvantage.

When one bird of paradise falls in love with another bird of paradise,
self-love comes under pressure to change into mutual admiration.
But often their egos cancel each other out
and they end up paralyzed inside an emotional vacuum.
Birds have been found locked in these trances up trees,
eyes as hard as diamonds.

A bird-watcher who waits in a cunningly constructed hide
to watch the mating display of *The Lonely Little King*
is doomed to be dazzled into a sense of sexual inadequacy.
Exquisite beauty of plumage makes the cock
one of the most perfect productions of Nature.
When he's ready for sex he just stands there.
The hen, overwhelmed and amazed,
faints clean away and wakes up ravished.

This same ornithologist may, if he recovers, see something
flash by like a brilliant thought – a completely phosphorescent bird.
It is *The Standard Wing*, also known as,
Wallace's Bird of Paradise.

It frequents the lower branches of virgin forests,
constantly in motion, clinging to vertical, smooth trunks
by means of luminary adhesion.
Food consists principally of photonic fruit,
June bugs, and glow-worms.
Safety sashes of fallen cyclists have been found
woven into the lighthouse-like nest of this bird.
Like the moth, or praying mantis, it is attracted to streetlamps,
circling the source of light with splendiferous outstretched wings.
A drunk of any religion coming home late at night who sees the universe
filtered through this glory will believe his end is near.

Only those with tenable delusions of their own grandeur
should risk encountering
The Superb Bird of Paradise.
These plumaged rhapsodies inhabit the part of New Guinea
called Serghile. Tribesmen catch them, wring their necks,
eviscerate the carcase, then dry the feathered skins
and take them to the trading store
to exchange for hatchets, coarse cloth,
and anthropological books about themselves.

When a biodiversity officer is dying somewhere
and starting to discover the limitations of agnosticism,
if the man has proved some use in life,
as a special blessing all the birds of paradise
flock to his mind.
As he dies in a state of technicolour bliss
they ride the thermal of his last breath.
This is the only time these feathered fables raise their voices in song.
To say the sound is of unearthly beauty
is to put the earth in better musical comparison
than it deserves.

In the early days of south-east Asian exploration,
language to describe these lovely wonders was not forthcoming.

The names Victorian gentlemen gave the birds
make one regret Gerard Manley Hopkins was not a traveller.
A specimen the natives called *The Bejewelled Playball
of the One-legged Creator*, became, in English,
merely *The Greater Bird of Paradise*.

The unusual feathers on the back of this bird
inflate when it reaches a certain height
thus making it easier for it to ascend.
The higher it gets, the bigger it becomes.
When it descends, it tries not to get smaller – but it does.
This bird is essentially a political life-form.
It should have been called
Ambition After an Election Defeat –
but words failed zoology.

As the good-looking girl hangs around with a plain friend,
the preferred companion of *The Greater Bird of Paradise*
is *The Lesser Bird of Paradise*.
But the Lesser Bird has a compulsion to perch on the
highest branch of the highest tree on the summit of the highest mountain.
If the Greater Bird goes up there it will burst.
So it remains at its safe level, gazing skywards, plaintively
puffed up and nowhere to go,
pining to be with its inferior.

When the Lesser Bird weakens with age
(so it is believed by the neolithic neck-
wringers of New Guinea), it flies off on its final journey,
driven by some Icarus-instinct
to roost in the flame-jungles of the sun.
Inevitably incinerated, its ash is sucked into orbit, tinting sunsets
for passengers in jumbo-jets whose fears
have been soothed by the simulations of the printed page.

London–Jakarta–Adelaide 1984

Family Reunion

We carry her ashes all the way from England in a paper bag.
　　Talk our way through Customs in boys' French –
　　　　Voilà les cindres de notre mère.
A breeze gets up from the cornfields of Africa,
enclouding the greyness we pour on his war-grave.

My brother was born posthumously – so this is the only time
　　　　we're all together as a family.
　　　　So, will you ever wash your hair again, brother?
　　　　Leave that for the rain – that same widowing,
wheat-kissing rain – a soldier's winter in these hills.

Quick, before the moment passes, we must leave,
　　　　and keep this hour perfect. Farewell
　　　　to the Army's dazzling, numbered headstone.
　　　　We tip the Islamic keepers of this quiet place
and run back into a day of our own making.

Madjez-el-Bab, Tunisia 1983

Working with Mary Ellen

Yes, I can see how, having written the play,
I'm the last person to understand it.
Your interpretration has more validity than mine.
You created the text through me from the beginning.
I might as well leave the rehearsal.

No, I'm not upset. The director has resigned anyway
and the other actors have gone to the pub.
Yes, you do know more about me
than I do myself – and yes, by all means,
cut those crap lines you've felt-penned in puce.

Your earthmotherliness…your Missouri
riverboat sense…your hazel eyes seeing through
all my verbal screens…your serene smile melting
the chain-mail of authorial pride… What chance have I got?
The play, and the playwright, are putty in your hands.

Of course I'll extend the section you like so much.
How many more lines d'you want? Sometimes I wonder
how you came by all this insightful power – then I remember
the runaway fifteen-year old who crossed America to act,
and the New York police sending you all the way home.

Off Hand

A certain stone stands in the herb garden,
barely a foot high, my name on it.
I made this part of the garden –
created it out of an old chicken run.

The stone disappears
each summer under oregano leaves,
hiding my name. I watch the slow action, the shade
on the stone growing in the best, most fruitful guise.
If I pick oregano I'm careful not to reveal the stone –
I leave it in the dark.

The stone was carved as part of a photo montage
for the dust-jacket of a novel
about Cathar masons, heretics hiding inside a system.
When the art editor was finished with the stone
she gave it me with a cheeky smile – this will save your heirs
having to pay for a monument.
It's already got your name on it.
The stone isn't all that hard.
Someone can scratch your dates on with a screwdriver.

I carried the stone home in doubled plastic *bags for life*,
which took the strain but stretched a little.
Each summer I sit close to where I know the stone is.
A sense of when I wasn't here,
and won't be here,
inevitably arrives.

Saint Briavels, 2005

Manuela Sáenz de Thorne

All that greatness, that change, that loving,
that refashioning
of a continent, spirals down
to one little woman rolling cigars
in memory of her lover, Bolívar.
Manuela, I am moved.

What did good manners ever matter
to a girl like you? What did public opinion ever matter
to a woman like you? What will death
ever matter to a beacon like you, blazing
desire beside the Pacific?

You are magnificent in the twilight of your first magnificence.
I credit myself far enough to say – like Satan fell in pride,
I'd have fallen for you,

QUARTET FOR GARETH

Perpetuum Mobile

He travelled widely as a child,
slept in a thousand landscapes,
great plains as blankets, purple
hills as pillows. Weeks of ocean
voyaging. Trains across the Kalahari.
Aircraft on their inter-continental
wires, shuttles on a Chinese loom.
In his youth and manhood, on he went –
the explorer strong within him,
risk and fear his chart
of ceaseless motion, writing
war and deprivation, seeking strangeness
in the lives of Syrian slaves,
rebels in an Ethiop cave,
Albanian hoods, Georgian dreamers,
loving skid row in Havana,
any contrabanded thought,
or underworld –
politics in Washington,
the drug scene of New York,
the central lock-up, New Orleans –
Then all these roads became too much.
The axle of his wheel hung
on the chassis of a shattered self.
I, the originator of his journeys,
now measure with the inch-tape
of a stricken mind every move he made,
every fraction of the earth he saw,
questioning, where has he been,
why did he go, where does he stand,
now he is dead.

Part Of It All

Your first time at the sea, in you went
until the waves came over your head.
At the solstice, when the sun
appeared to stand still in the sky,
you went under the great stones
to became part of their stillness
and part of it all.

You've left me eclipsed, wondering
where to go in this time.
You took my place
and I'm here in your future
asking – what would he have done
with this life, worked in what way
to remain part of it all?

Death reversed the natural order
leaving the old
where the young should be,
and this night is long, my son.
If your wild star shone out of my darkness,
redeeming my part of it all,
I could see how to live.

Midsummer's Day, 2004

Ynys Enllis

I have brought you in mind to this isle.
Those who could not love the world
came here, prayers for liberation
like your own frozen on their lips.
In death they numbered twenty thousand.

I have found somewhere to keep you;
have settled on this resting-place
– home for that second self
you sought, the pure man finding
peace at the ocean's edge.

The powerful current funnelled
between the isle and the mainland,
is so like the strait of your spirit.
Without turbulence, you drifted,
ash from your own precocious flame.

When I sail away and leave you here,
the goddess we both recognised
will watch over you. Remember her?
Teacher, lover, judge and sister,
mother of more than smiling harlotry.

She wears no halo of cocaine;
no mention of eureka in her speech.
She is essence, your seeking mind.
The time left over from tuition,
she'll spend weaving me a shawl of grief.

Grey seals loll here, sheep with fleece
of startling white blend with the birds above.
Pilgrims arrive in boats, embracing
the end of things, as I must the end
of all our talk – the loss that brought me here.

The boat comes in – you look up
from my sorrow. Guilt at your going
flings me back to ancient punishments.
Your hubris must be met with judgement
or we lose your beauty.

Loss makes its own magic.
You become that cormorant over there,
drying black wings in the sun.
Its plumage shimmers with your rainbow blaze,
neck twisted in a question-mark,

You always had the power
to metamorphose, shifting your ground
as doors opened in perceptions.
Now, by a different change, you exorcise
my horror at the waste.

A unique apple has been bred here,
fruit salt-tasting like a tear. Its habit
is to climb. An old father showed me
his leaf-covered house, regretting
how he'd let its growth get out of hand.

I will find a son of this climber, plant it
by the wall of my work-place, praying
its roots strike deeper than all sadness.
When it threatens to obscure my window,
I'll prune it – the lightest of touches.

We are called to the boat by a tin trumpet.
The pilgrims bid adieu to their rehearsals.
If I return some day and cannot find
my cormorant, I'll know you've flown
to where the fish are shoaling and the sea is clear.

Avebury Ring

So, for the solstice, you went
to celebrate life amongst great stones –
impressive in their statement of indestructibity
(though the power-shovel is parked behind trees).
As you travelled there, I see you happy,
wearing your sweet-sour smile,
pleased to be surrounded by a mystery
which we agreed to call mankind in you.

At first light, you rose
and welcomed in the special day.
Throughout the hours, you drank
and drank to wisdom.

With dusk descending, answers evading you –
you slept in a field,
something one can still do at forty,
just about, if your woman is watching over you
and death is no more than daisies crushed
beneath your hip.

Thinking About Moving

Through the gap in the wall,
into the big field the beast passes.
How long will it stay here?
What dominion will it accept?

Time is a declining mercy.
Exploration of great hills and springs
underground may have to be left aside
in favour of rich grass.

Meanwhile there are these acres
of enclosed, twisted sunlight. Trees
with moving shade follow the course
of greening fruit. But soon we must go.

Enna

Here, according to myth
and Milton, was the neck
of the wine-pot of Hell.

From this brackish lake
emerged the gloomy, foaming
Lord of Wrong, eyes grey

as phlegm, yearning for light.
He was fortunate. Dis grabbed
his woman amid brilliant flowers,

while we, folk from afar,
found a snarling race-track
and the Bar Proserpina del'Autocar.

Portability

For ten years the faceless stone-age folk
of this island have worshipped you:
females wear coiled fossils of your beauty
at their throats, men yearn for you like sea-caves.

The past has you for company
in my dreaming; you are haunter of groves
and hills, dryad in a mist of golden leaves.
I sleep mythfully because of your unpresence.

High stones I erect in your honour,
fierce taboos I create, rituals erupt nightly.
Carried here as an idol of the mind,
when I leave, your cult goes with me.

Calan Porter, 1984

Night Ferry

Sea and sky are interchangeable
Until the rising sun
Identifies the earthcraft line
That separates them.
The yawning passenger has spent
A hard night out on deck,
Wanting to dream beneath unusual stars,
To forget the land. He wakes
Inside the rolling night and searches
For some point of recognition.
Lost at sea. Where am I?
Only white light hesitating in the wings
Of seagulls tells him where.
That is the sea. This is the sky.
Wait for the sun.
                         As it breaks the line
He re-asserts his hold upon
The broad frames of the universe,
Re-adjusts his view of heaven,
Breathes again. In sleep his journey
Has carried him onwards. All is trust.
The trail of diesel smoke across the dawn
Says – you have moved.
                              The passenger remembers
Ancient tribes thought help was given
To the sun to burst out of the holding sea
By chanting *go* and *fly* and *rise*.
The passenger priests up his soul
With these encouragements, and lo,
The sun obeys.
                    The island lies beneath
The day's blaze as though born from this success.
When the passenger sets foot he'll find
Groves snowing with butterflies,

Air that sways with rosemary,
Cattle that sing, not bawl,
So blessed is this place. Orchards will be
White with almond blossom. Oranges
Will hang in grey mossed-up trees, life
Bulging out of cemetery sides. But the island
Has not the sanctity of the sea,
The sacredness of the sea,
The healing power of the salt,
Seamless sea.
                      Although the passenger
Will find rapture on the island,
It will be of the shallower sort
With huge grasshoppers leaping goldenly,
Ticking terrapins nosing, swifts swooping,
Naked men and women hiding in the rocks
Unsure of their beliefs. Once on the island
After a basin or two of earthen thoughts, he will
Be back to the sea, searching
For shoaling fish, watching for dolphins
Splitting whirlpools with bronze cleavers,
Scallops praying tightly on the sand.
He will swim to find shelter from the storm
In sea-caves studded with bubbles.
He will stand beneath cliffs and let the rain
Running off the edge lave his body, accepting
The pain of small stones.
He will note how the thunder-cloud over the sea,
Looms austere and serious as a saint
Before becoming a bully over the land.
In a deserted cove
He'll find millions of beach balls
Blown from the hands of sporting youths
Throughout the Mediterranean Sea.
The black stuff on the passenger's feet will be

Tears such lads shed for the cold of girls
Who never played ball.
                    There is the coast.
The passenger sees towers
Lighthouses, cliffs, roads and rocks, the white heaps
Of sunning houses. Here comes the harbour mouth
To swallow the smoking ship.
He sees the ancient fort, the gun-emplacements,
The lazar-house for lepers, the islet put aside
For quarantine, the dim grey warship snoozing
In its slip. Over the land are rectangles of roads.
Soldiers march. Tanks trundle – playing
Franco's geriatric games. The passenger would rather
Stay outside those rows of teeth, not disembark,
And sail eternally around the island, washing it
Clean with words.
                    Here is a city.
Ropes are thrown to bind the ship to the land.
A different smell comes through the porthole
As he packs.
                    The passenger seeks microcosms,
Has been to islands where the natives do not know
The names of simple flowers, but can recite
The Army list by heart. These people, in their blasted
Innocence left priests to baptize honeysuckle,
Rose and weed.
                    This island has become ignorant
Of its inner nature. The soil accepts
All flowering identities. Host has become
Visitor. His house, the point
From which all guests departed.
Only the sea remains as it was, though poisoned.
But the victim of a toxic force still has a dignity
Within antidotes and faith in the future.
The passenger will lie prostrate

Before the altar of the poisoned sea,
Making libations of holy oil, reading
Liturgies in trashy books, the flotsam
Of the corrupted mind.
                              He will worship
The unchangeable while his body changes
In hue – verdigris and bronze, as if his skin
Were stretched across the bottom of the sea.
And his brain, oh, his brain, will be encrusted
With the glorious scum of Paradise.

Caldy War Memorial

So many names, so many movements
    of the hand,
my blood is dashed and drawn
    upon this rock,
his love struck out
    above the estuary
where, pink and delicate,
    the feet of seabirds
torment the even sands with words:
my buried one, so shaken
by the pounding of the tide.

This is the mood and mould
    of yesterdays,
the son awake to what has been forgotten –
    and every love I have
comes from the splendours of that dying man,
    my father.
I see him torn above
    the grey draught of the sky
to what is not his heaven;
then he, like everyone,
is lost until tomorrow.

Hotel Costa da Sol

From this baking hotel bedroom
you can hear the slow slave's
laughter in the sea. Drowsy on dreams
you follow its swaying
as it seduces the Indian wind.

Here, alone on an empty pillow,
the resident lies restless,
receiving the transmissions
of sex-starved men who sleep
upon the nearby prison island.

Bodies hard as anthracite
burn up dreams of women: arab dhows
sail masted past their cells, waked in lust.
All this tourist dreams is swift escape
from love's imprisonment.

Mocambique, 1965

Audrey at Ninety

Pouring down from the granite moors
the stream brokenly mirrors your wood –
fast-running memory carrying reflections.

When the vixen drinks, head between paws,
at her habitual place, she remembers her young
and all she must do to live freely.

The sweat of quarrymen prising a church
out of the earth salts raindrops globed on leaves,
the crystal ball of endless labour.

In the sounds of the wood are boys
sharpening tools for fathers, carrying
water, fruit and wood for mothers.

Entering your memory I see a distant man
standing very still, a bird upon his finger,
knowing it is only with him for a while.

The stream does not leave what it flows over.
Once seen, images become part of the mirror.
Life does not leave us – we follow where it's been.

The Shrine at Siguena

No use looking helpless in Aragon:
the red emptiness does not bring up fellow-feeling.
You can stand in a ruined courtyard,
miles from anywhere, looking like a man from outer space
but the nuns will go on tinkering with the tractor,
perplexed by divine wilfulness within machinery.
No stranger is as real as a starter motor,
nor will nosiness ever plough a field.

But they sent out a novice to deal with me.
She was slight, still in girlhood, carrying clasped
to her breast a long, ferruginous key.
She opened the ancient doors
as if they were arms:
she put on the lights
as if they were thoughts:
she led me into the old church
as if it swarmed with brilliant verities:
she showed me the tomb

of King Pedro the Licentious –
huge, blunted sandstone slabs jammed together,
thighs at a giants' orgy, all adornment and epitaph
eaten away, looming in a vaulted corner.
She laid one hand upon the tomb, leaning,
like an odalisque, her smile replete with understanding
of this driven monarch, long since
cured of his compulsions.
Outside, her sisters got the tractor going.
My guide ran out to join them,
leaving me alone with Pedro's dust,
long key left in the door.

The Setting of Nets

The man who owns this boat has painted eyes
upon the bows, not trusting Marx to soothe a storm.
They stare down through the sea, superstitious pilots
steering this old communist around Athenian wrecks –
wooden eye-lids creaking, tear-ducts leaking.

This early morning I beheld the boatman
as he played his cornet in the crowded square
in memory of partisans. He squeezed his salty lips
against the mouth of brassy Aphrodite, blowing
sex into a revolutionary scream. Heroic dream.

His broad face slants against the sun, Slavonic, gold
and grizzled; while at the bow his student son says
all philosophy inclines towards the unexplained.
Father lets these spinning hooks of words trail in our wake
unbaited, lures for predators and Lenin's creditors.

There is one species we will catch, I know; a round fish
having the expression of an outraged Roman emperor under
the assassin's sword. The morning will come lightly;
we will lift our nets, raising these imperial clowns
in strangling strings. Beautiful things.

The son would like to visit England. Don't! breathes
the boatman. That's where the Sirens sing their endless
profit dialogue with Socrates. They're not the only ones –
Odysseus calls, Circe and Calypso were never short of
man's immortal money – cynic's Soviet Christian honey.

We pause, pay out the net around a circle of bright swelling
sand. Tomorrow, after breakfast in the easy wind of olive
leaves, we'll come again in half-speech, half-understanding,
rowing hard to see what we have caught and drowned
beneath the moon. A siren is a warning, not a tune.

Turning for the port we see white puffs of smoke shoot
from the limestone mountains, then explosions roll across
the settling sea. Father instinctively reacts, reaching for a gun
that once was there, and searches the horizon for grey Huns
coming to take his blood to slave. Son, watch for that wave.

Do not go to England. Do not waste so many years of careful
thought. There is the boat, my books, my courage – stay!
Upon the mountain dynamiters push their drilling-rig against
the rock. The compressed air of freedom makes a rapid road.
The son dives angrily to the depths inside. Watch him glide.

Budva, Yugoslavia, 1977

Blind Girl on Cattolica Beach

Dragged streaming from the sea,
a beautiful, slender, sightless fish,
she trailed along behind her anxious mother,
unwilling to leave an element she understood.

Neptune's daughter, groping spirit,
amphibian soul, gasping over boy-blitzed sand,
her gleaming scales and rapturous flesh,
amazing Saxon men from Vandal-land.

Images of burning ships and towers,
of barbarous rape committed on a darkened queen,
seared her, then the hot wind from the sea
licked her soul to tears.

Cobweb in the Eye of an African Mask

The spider moved on
leaving you this blinder.
The arachnid is pale and clever,
sporting an outside poison sac,
outspinning everybody
with a foot in six continents.

Wipe your eye.

Museum Piece

The river-god Akragas knows when to come and when to go
        and when to disappear entirely,
causing drought to vines and corn, digging the dry grave
        of his own divinity.
Of all natural features of the landscape he has the most
        beauty and form, the most
beginning, the most middle, the most end. He is subject
        to the moment of change
and can be seen in the shape of a man, as here in this old
        unearthed object. Both crumble,
shard and citizen, both can be preserved by artificial means,
        dams, reservoirs and walls.

The river-god Akragas shouted hey and ho and thundered
        in his anger, or shone
a long and rolling smile along the valleys troubled
        by the settlements of man.
He was lord of all which stirring moves, stirring dies,
        and all that rises,
king of the shining pebble, dwarf of the shrunken cloud,
        for the storm made him, and made
his power while the storm in man fingered this earthen pot
        to make his face, curl his beard
and show a god of occasional strength whose whole existence
        was a rhythmical, seasonal sway.

The river-god Akragas could be flooded, soaked with happiness
        or painfully starved
until his bowels latched to his backbone. He could leap like
        an athlete with thunderbolts
in his hands, or lie flat on his back in old age, meandering.
        Sad, he is generally forgotten now
as rivers flow unholy, but in this quiet room of a summer
        palace turned museum, he has a place
in trays of gods who failed. Something in his eye – a bit
        of blue – reminds me of rebirth and rain.

Villanelle

During days of spectral grey
when love's pleasures seem so scarce,
we must find them where we may.

All our fortunes seem at bay,
as if earth had lost her purse,
vagrant dressed in rags of day.

How can winter not dismay,
blast our blessings into curse,
while we crave green April, May?

Only in the blood this day
can be filled earth's threadbare purse,
gold your eyes, not coiner's grey.

Lovers find the means to pay
passion's wages from what's worse –
let the age steal what it may.

Now the frozen birds will play,
flowers bedeck a winter hearse,
years ahead we'll have to pay
but look, this February is May.

That Hat

At the registry office
I thought I'd been sent the wrong bride.
Later, as we walked
the streets of Stratford with our wedding-guests,
I kept looking under that hat
to see who you were.
Encountering your eyes and smile,
I was only partially assured –
Why was this lovely woman I loved,
disguised as an alien?

Since then I've been haunted
by that hat, that felt chapeau
shaped like a mutant oyster.
Sometimes I take it
off the top of the wardrobe
blow off the dust and wonder
if I binned the thing, you'd notice.

Why did you wear it?
Where did you find it?
Perhaps your mother
left it to you in her will –
whenever marrying,
wear this magic helmet.

Instinct

The human mind packed
into a cylinder of the spirit
blackpowder ego fuse waiting
kind of cartridge with brains.

The subtlety of books lost
upon the locust – scribed
pages chewed in mistake
for leaves, wisdom ignored.

Philosophy to the shrew
peaceful and earthy.
Cats computer fast and clawed
with room for cruel, cruel play.

Sons who must kill fathers,
brothers who hate brothers –
this being Nature's motherboard,
find me another.

Pollyjoke Beach

In cold sea surf a boy bathes alone,
an arrow in the drawn bow of the tide.

Warlike in his fantasies, eager in his ecstasies,
he glows in the chill salt, not conscious of the cold.

Waves beat upon his flesh, tides pull him,
huge gulls bracket his unknowing mind.

Knowledge of joy burns in his eye,
glows on his skin, sounds in his cry.

Child-minder

This is a spark born of a bated brilliance
which was never born, a child we lost and tried again.
Closely I watch him play, observing
his existence with a heavy kind of pride,
and when it rains I usher him inside, inside.

In a second room I hung on begging for his birth,
remembering the other spark that faded out,
refusing flat to father me.
I was an atom of its lifelessness
and the aborted orbited my restlessness.

Now this boy is here for brief enough a time
before he moves away to burnings of his own.
What he will look for, how his mind will fire,
are deeply dreamt by me in deepening hours
while years within create a garden's powers.

He'll saunter through these rooms, eat here,
sleep there, wash in that bowl,
stalk through this garden, humble every tree,
share all my windows looking out on earth
then turn to look and guess my worth.

Brother, sister, mother, wait upon him best,
know Tom is last to come and first to be.
He takes this eminence as natural while I,
to shield him from the sun's hot glare,
keep cool his soul with every kind of care.

Max

At the moment of birth
your expression changed with each blink
of a star-blue-eye, as if you were trying
out characters, or, impatient with the time
mental processes take, you were hurrying
on to the next new feeling.

Speed was important to you
from the beginning – you jumped into my hands
like a man escaping from a skyscraper in flames.
Now you're steadying up, but still
push forward hungrily,
needing to prove you're here.

The effects of your dazzling entry
have died down. You occupy a slower frame of being.
When speech comes, banal it may be,
but we'll listen closely to what you say
in case it bears a coded message
from where the unborn store our secrets.

Astronauts

Too many nights have these Americans
searched the sky for the lunar probe
splashing down
in this, their patch of ocean –
even though the naked eye
would never catch its fall.
They wish all astronauts in heaven
and themselves at home.

In this coral inlet, protected
by a booming reef, we play cards
and chat while they await
the call that never comes.

Black paramatics in their diving suits,
each day they train and train, foetal
in the belly of a giant mother plane,
hoping those shot into space
will take their cue to tumble down again.

Sitting here in the candlelight
these long-held men can't find a smile
for the suavery of the *maître d*,
from the consommé unto the Brie
there's a floor-show of *ennui*.

The menu can't deflect them
from looking upwards for a sign –
a sign to send them hurtling through the night
to find a capsule and two star-crossed men
so history can start again.

A pause, a laugh, their fingers point
up at the rafters – we look along the line,
to catch a cane-rat as he orbits
through his prime, then arrogantly strolls
back down to earth intact and fat.

Mauritius, 1965

TWO SONNETS

To a Secretary

You've not noticed me go walking
past your office window; it faces east
and I walk west to the water's ring,
and the rising fly that fools the beast.
So we have never come together face to face
or flesh to flesh. Whatever attributes
you have, your unseen grace,
are lost on me, a blur which suits
spirits of my sort. Your truth exists
only by risking existence in my dream.
You're the phantom type I can't resist –
to have you I need never plot or scheme,
but go on drifting lakewards past your glass
to fish – thus may all my faithless visions pass.

Effigy

Tudor gent and wife, her nose over his shoulder,
as if recalling in a rhapsody his body-odour,
rest full-length on their tomb, ruffed and gowned.
Passing the long time, she smiles, he frowns,
stiffly propped upon clumsily carved elbows,
watching television dust dance in the windows.
Centuries ago, Puritan image-breakers
left them ears to be deaf with, a show
of eyes to be blind – signs of the senses,
cured of all futile, eternal pretences;
but they vandalized limbs, bruised flesh
of desire, hot hands, running feet.
Garish old paintwork, so far off the mark,
endured mutilation. Let them dream in the dark.

Saint Briavels, 2004

Longsleddale Eagle

Having discussed her with learning
we meandered where the river showed us
    an uphill way towards its rushing
source. Many had come to see her, twitchers
    hung on the hours in hope of glimpsing
beauty in suspended power,
    half-birds, half-men, dumb as thrushes
facing death in the shadow of her wings.

In this rough landscape more have witnessed
storms and hell than watched her pass; seen ghosts
    legging the snow-clad fell
than viewed the golden saucers of her eyes.
    She scorns the mob, the gilded town,
rejecting aid, tearing science on every side,
    wearing the exile's crown of rarity,
aloof, ominous, alone – a symbol in the sky.

We walked the fells until the dusk
was coming down, eye-tired and fagged.
    Sitting by a fall we listened to the river
as it rinsed the stony pass.
    Then she came, low and quiet,
huge in questioning contempt –
    infertile though my sacred egg may be,
what kind of prey is this? Defecating,
    she sailed on to hunt the final glow of day.

Out of Mammon

for Glyn Hughes

One of those days when optimism
surges because the weather's bright
saw yours truly searching for a present
for a gardenless friend at a garden centre,
hoping against hope, as he does.

Hosts of gnomes, monsters, granite muses,
gargoyles, cupped hands, Donald Duck sundials,
lapidary junk, undermined the good mood.
Giving up, I turned towards the exit,
annoyed at bad taste's empire.

Then I saw a cast half-hidden behind
a giant foot. Amongst the kickshaws
it possessed grace, style, meaning
and dignity. This has been put in my way,
I thought. My friend shall have it.

Here is his eolithic mind winding round itself,
sunk in ancient seas that have disappeared,
building up poems out of lime and quartz,
whorls looking inwards but opening
outwards, always opening outwards.

There was no tag on it. I took it to the desk,
computer lists were checked, no record found.
Where the ammonite came from was a mystery.
What should they charge? As the one true form
in the place, it was priceless.

Four poems set to music by Sally Beamish for the King's Singers

Porin' Trow

On the day we moved in
we stood in the road
admiring our house
having stripped off its ivy
in a frenzy of change

Coming out of his door
to see who we were
he walked to his gate
and extended his hand
gave a biblical name

You're changing the ways
bending the ways
O the old ways
but whatever you do
you're just porin' trow

Porin' trow? Porin' trow?
Yes, just porin' trow.
Say that slowly for us
So we'll understand
what you're saying

Stranger, whatever you do
you're just pouring through
like all of us do
pouring through
pouring through
like all of us do

Weather Report

In forest rain fugitives gather
funghi below trees,
spores sail upwards
past leaves seeking sun
in the free, unhindered sky.

Through forest snow come the detectives
tracking down murderers,
following prints published
by bloody feet, bodies
speechless in drifts.

By forest wind the sweet air's combed.
Oaks planted in paradise shake
over the graves of angels.
Spores, prints and blood
end up in the eyes of Adam and Eve.

Walk in the Forest

Within the eye, these wooded hills seem heightless.
Their shade is everything, their quiet, our thoughts
As we walk up not noticing the slope.

We foot the rising ground beneath the leaves.
Oak and fern, oak and fern, huge age and tender green.
Foxgloves raise their toxic spires, triumphant.

The land swells up in secret, catching unaware
The wanderers threading silent through the trees
Who wonder why their hearts beat harder.

The summit is a glade in open sunlight.
We cannot see the greater world for branches.
Within the eye, these wooded hills seem heightless.

New Year at the Dump

Unwanted Christmas presents poignantly new
in late afternoon light – an exercise cycle
(Me, overweight? Never been so insulted
in my life!) The centrifugal vacuum cleaner –
(You'll never teach me to be houseproud.)
The motor mower that lost the will to live.
The sauna kit that cooked the owner to a
turn. But not in plastic bags, if you please.

Computers that have argued back too often.
Baby chairs encrusted with the pulp of fruit.
Strange plastic chairs to fit a hippo's rear.
Mountains of glass which glitter with a glacial
smile – drink is as wearing as geological time.
In the shelter of the skip for corrugated cardboard only
stand dead batteries, spent chemicals and garden
waste. But not in plastic bags, if you please.

Mattresses of dream and birth, of giving up the ghost.
Albums, treasured imprints of our family life.
Paper, paper, paper, snowflakes written on –
Yours sincerely, truly, ever, almost, see you, farewell,
Gone. It took us twenty years to find the guts
To throw away what now awaits the pomp of burial
By bulldozer. But not in plastic bags, if you please.
Not in plastic bags

Another Country

A small port on the eastern side of Italy
was where we made our marriage bed:
tired from champagne and a three-hour flight
we made some love, lay down our head.

She fell asleep in that sea-smelling room,
moon pouring through slats in the shutter,
I lay awake, too wired up to sleep –
Heard her breathe, heard her dream, heard her mutter.

I lay there for hours in the silver-lined cloud,
far away from all passionate errors,
regardless of every low trick of the heart
as two minds search the truth for one mirror.

When dawn doused the moon I opened
the window to have a good look at the sea;
across a broad strait was a coast, not expected,
a harbour, boats, hills covered with trees.

Surprised, I attempted to waken my wife,
but she wouldn't emerge from her sleep;
closing the shutters I went back to bed,
bemused how our map could mislead.

We slept till the sounds of the beach and the town
rolled into the room with the heat:
we showered and waited for coffee to come
and met as most manage to meet.

This map is all wrong. I showed her the place,
a straight north/south line, A to B,
take a look for yourself from the terrace, my love –
there's the coast of another country.

She rose and went out, stepping into the sun –
from the brightness she shielded her eyes.
Quiet and sad, she said nothing was there,
my mirage forerunning a life-time of lies.

1962

Regular War

For years I lived along a road
bisected by the route of elephant,
the line of their mysterious migrations
from Lozi land up to the Congo hills.
Once a year they came, and then returned
in brawling, grey divisions, quite unstoppable:
like tanks they passed us by at night,
their ivory headlamped with stars,
and we could hear their vast bowels rumbling,
huge engines in the dark.

In the morning, once again defeated,
we roamed the battleground of bush
and trampled gardens, collecting cannon-balls
to raise some cabbages, fodder
for their next campaign.

Croc

From a concrete bridge
over the Kafue river
you were observed, *ngandu*,
sleeping with your mouth open

causing chaos on the Congo road.

What an easy time, straddling
a mudbank, gob wide
to attract
witless river-life

to your chieftain gullet.

It's no wonder, O wingless
aberration of a flying reptile,
the men on the bridge dub you king –
all jaws and no kissing,

all take and no giving.

Lying in State of an African Liberation Hero

The shoes for the funeral horses
the steel for the funeral stone
the blow for the funeral curses
the dog for the funeral bone
the light for the funeral darkness
the sheet for the funeral bed
the breast for the funeral harness
the crown for the funeral head
the rope for the funeral pulley
the tear for the funeral eye
the blood for the funeral weather
the breath for the funeral sigh
the creak for the funeral floor-board
the snap for the funeral string
the wine for the funeral heartache
the bee for the funeral sting
the sum for the funeral number
the link for the funeral chain
the hand for the funeral handshake
the ball for the funeral game.

The Rape of Leda

"Who am I?" whispered the greatest of gods
crammed into a cob's body so he could have
the king of Sparta's wife.

"Some bird," replied the laconical queen,
then, more talkatively as he trod,
"You'll get nothing faked."

"Come fly with me," Zeus breathed jovially,
waving his pinions in the air, ecstatic,
"let yourself go."

"Not a chance," she said, struggling, sinking,
suffocating in his male plumage,
"after this you'll get no reverence from me."

So Zeus punished her hard, grounding,
grinding, flapping, sowing her womb
with three adulterous daughters

who'd make nothing but trouble.
Then he pecked her cheek and thrashed off,
leaving soft down everywhere.

The Valley of Temples

Birds yellow and black sing in these ruined temples.
No attempt at harmony is made, part-singing is roughly
pushed aside to make way for the raucous ritual of mating.
The song becomes a roar of change, a battle-cry.

Pillared in brown limestone, proof of sea-bed balance
are these pagan places – now rebuilt as postcard images
sought by a thousand cameras. We view, shutter, marvel
how this glory passed away, then listen to the fighting birds.

Here young brides come from churches in the hilltop town,
carnations sellotaped over the bonnets of black wedding cars.
Donna, thy dark husband could be Phoenician, Greek,
Saracen or Roman – even Norman-French in blood.

Hold still. A smile. The couples mount the altar steps
and pose within the framework of a famous harmony,
standing on the sacrificial stone of Concord. All pray
as pagans. Widows eye these fallen pillars, curse these
broken gates.

Agrigento, Sicily, 1976

FOUR VALENTINES

They say love's all heart,
　　love is arrows,
love's there for us all,
　　field-mice and sparrows –
love's a rambling rose
　　also an herb –
love's a stretch limousine
　　parked up on the kerb.

Love's a closely-kept secret
　　behind transparent doors,
a point of debate between
　　policemen and whores –
an improbable yarn
　　in a hidebound edition –
a truth that withdraws
　　to escape definition.

Unsplittable diamond
Found beside a flooding river
In the red Devon earth,
Pass everything I do
Through your refracting light
For that flood has got inside me.

Broken houses, paper, plays,
Books, wars, treaties, victims,
All are carried in my head
Of channel-seeking water.
Only the indivisible can show
The best way seawards –
Yours is the only bed I know.

Look, ignore my first note.
Don't wait to ring.
Just stop what you're doing
And come to bed.
My room is right over here.
I'll take the waders off, of course.
Dazzling is usually over
In an instant but I've a feeling
Years from now I'll still
Be shielding my eyes.

Love leads me strangely through the wood,
each day, a glade, each action branching
with no history attached except blind roots,
unreasoned except in blood and hours with you.

Those hours are trees regenerating light
stored in their leaves. The sun may go but gold
pours in the dark when we dream in separate worlds
holding our breath on instants, unable

to look back to find the path trodden
getting us here. When the edge of the wood
is reached, don't give me the kiss
of tomorrow – give me the kiss of today, today.

Christmas Eve at Lady Margaret's Church

Flowers are being arranged at the altar
    for Parliament's prayers.
Out of season blooms browbeat the stump
    of the all-night sitting candle,
illuminating the unheard debate:
    Render unto Caesar sundered the faith
before it got off the ground.

The tower booms with impersonations
    of division bells sounding over another lost cause –
some obscure, pensionable issue
    emptying the chamber.

Christ (forever the back-bencher), is on his feet,
    to a deserted House, re-crucified.
Hanging round the Commons bars,
    would bring him more disciples
than waiting here in this gloom for a front-bench job
    which would give his myrrhed, fantastic tongue
the clout of well-arranged
    chrysanthemums.

Westminster, 1986

Flies

The flies sit bright upon the summer leaf,
safe in a green-veined hand, asleep
before they start the ritual of remove,
searching the world to find that holy groove.
They've raped the orchard, mounted sweetheart flowers,
fizzed erotically through every summer bower;
for further sex, ravished the grass and fucked the stream,
buggered our strawberries and made love to the cream –
I must find a book or paper
To stop this most licentious caper.

While I search round, their fornication
hums – two electric motors mating.
I have a hand, in fact I've two,
also a shirt, a hat, a shoe.
No urge of cruelty propels me to the buzzing pair
that lie in ecstasy upon a striped deck-chair –
my aim is peace. I terminate their life
locked up in love, the man within his wife;
then I continue with my picnic tea
sombre in thought – one day desire might flatten me.

Pèlerinage d'un Jour

Lourdes, steep town of an expensive deity,
arch-whore, tasselled harlot, holy spiv, gilt trader
in the Temple, lifting godhead, maidenhead,
nearly dead to the cure of a virgin scared by a virgin
in a cave, the thunder of the mum of God
demanding and promising miracles.
                                      Sitting in wheelchairs,
lying in beds beneath the trees, the sick
listen to the loudspeaker Latin, the stiff nurses
beside them the sentries of cure –
                          a spectacle
you might find in some sunny corner
of a run-down zoo where sloths
are being encouraged to mate with panthers.

Fire in the Touraine

So sleep we, wined
like marinated meat,
boys bunged together
in the wrestling heat
of this chevalier summer,

snoring, creating amours
from dark doubts and dreams,
aglow with chateaux,
footsore from following
girls round the park, we rest.

Below, in the basement,
a stripper unfurls
in the sun's hoarded heat –
Are our teachers in there
champagne at the lip?

As we lie in seed mood,
swopping heaven and hell,
a spark from an obsolete fan
ignites the old wooden hotel
and we burn in our beds.

Four pure virgin boys
die in the blaze – they fall
through the core of the flame
right past the ghost
of the stripper's cold gaze.

Saved, not reduced
to celibate ash, we return
to our land. As my mother
inhales the smoke on my clothes
she cries out in fear.

Torben

Your DNA never left the Danelaw.
One night in Stamford town spirits
of Eric Bloodaxe, Ivar of the Broad Embrace
and Ragnar Hairy Breeks gamed
your skaldic genes out of the box,
decided the long-handled axe
should swing in your writing brain,
imposed the code of the shieldless berserker
who must fight armoured only in rage.

Up the muddy estuary of this deluded
kingdom your long ship noses,
dragon prow snarling through the fog.
Alarm bells ring in the hapless towers,
the witless bury their gold in dungheaps,
victims rehearse pleas of poverty and pain.
Another raid by the Viking playwright
cometh, burning suburbs to the ground.
Your plunder makes a city without walls.

Photographs

There are some shots of you
we keep shuffled in with all the rest –
old prints of travels, friends
sitting round a table raising glasses –
you know the kind of thing I mean;
flashbacks where your life has been.

But these are different: they
were taken at a killing time
when our inseparable ways lay torn
asunder. The mind behind the shutter's
blink, the fingerprint that took you there,
is nameless, but occupies a lair

of memory. These pictures make
me think of being free again.
Your smile is soft. The sky is clear.
You seem relaxed and better placed
to find yourself. Behind you is a figure
in a landscape where I never went –
he looks away, his jealousy is spent.

The Ilala

After a long estrangement we sat
upon the ancient steamer's upper deck,
voyaging round an inland sea,
to rebuild the heart's wreck.

For seven days we sailed past islands,
shores thronged with naked children,
cathedrals made of corrugated iron,
kapenta fishers. Women penned

in the hold, sang songs of battles
as they gave suck. At table we shared
food with missionaries so drunk
the names of gods and common birds

escaped them. In radiant air, Eric the
Danish engineer, held over the side to puke
into the moonstruck lake, outlined the Africa
effect: too big, too old to respect, great cycles,

vastness equals lostness. Live in smaller,
saner places. At the end of our round trip
we were unloaded back onto the quay as
undelivered cargo. Peace names this ship.

Lake Malawi, 1968

Incident at the Theatre

Such a crowd is here.
                Good to see these old benches
thronged again. Electra enters masked in
                grief, her hollow eyes
a drought of tears. Her nylon cloak
                attracts the dust magnetically
in dionysian dance while wild Orestes
                in aluminium armour,
raves in Greek, a warrior cooked in kitchen foil.
                Now these thoughts perish
banished by an uproar in the stalls – a hundred
                special policemen turn
to watch a tourist stoned climb on the stage.
                He spits on skene
and panaskenia, every angle
                of this chiselled maze.
"Far out!" he yells. "Too much!
                You've blown my mind for me.
This stuff is lies, not even history."

Epidaurus, Greece, 1966

Letter from Michelangelo's Moses

(written on the day he was finished)

Dear God,
       Bushes of fire and ocean carving aside,
and in spite of knowing how you (even in your
ambiguity) hate puns, I'd like to have a go at art.
It is image-making, I acknowledge, and contrary
to the commandments – but we must modernize,
and it is strictly for the sake of furthering religion.

       Using chips from that mad fellow's mallet,
and garnet, malachite and sundry coloured bits, thy
sacred laws could be written out again on floors
for folk to walk on.

       A text laid out beneath the feet means sapience
rises through the balls of balance. The pun I'll leave
to your imagination.

       Give me authority to spell thy meaning
out on horizontal planes, where mankind likes to lie.
The great stone tablets haven't served their purpose.
Let man look down upon your laws between his toes,
not struggle to construct load-bearing libraries
for those almighty slabs.

       I will learn the craft of making truth out
of fragments, piece by piece, laying out thy mind in strong
cement as our foundation – a lithomantic explication
any child can understand.

       So, if the idea appeals, O Lord,
don't let them put me in Saint Peter's, Rome
to stand in idleness, essential work undone.
Down on these quarried knees I'll daily go to
set this holy pavement in the common street.

Provide me with the fission in my fists to
emulate my maker, Angelo. I know his cutting edge.
I know his rage. I know his heart, his strokes,
his pounding. His spirit is the twin of mine.
Reveal, reveal, in shattered stone.
I wait to hear.

Angoni Burial

A lone white man amongst the funeral crowd,
perspiring epitaph for a miner's fall
into a grave that took him twenty years
to dig and five minutes to fill.

Outside my bones I am official
representative, speech-maker of sorrow
for a distant management. My oratory
is paid for and my tongue is mercenary.

Red dust covers the crowd, a prince's cloak
of mourners dragging up the hill. The colour
is old Africa's; the blood drained off
black regiments and chieftains slaughtered.

The dust now covers him and me, both
in our box, both listening to his wife
who beats her empty breasts and keens
her endless, time-accustomed song.

What can I sing, not understanding
half his rudimentary thoughts?
Angoni sleeper in your L-shaped grave,
no earth falls straight upon you

from the spade, unlike my ignorance.

Nchanga, 1965

Gulliver's Holiday Disaster

He woke on the beach,
part of a two-thousand room hotel –
the five-star *Majestic*,
Mediterranean fast building at its best.

Decorative palms
planted overnight in his nostrils,
children's railway up his trouser leg,
navel now a jacuzzi, nails
made into snooker tables, eyeballs
water-beds and his
crutch a conservatory.

Muzak piped through his dining area
gave him a digestive disorder –
which was fortunate for all,
for it meant he durst not fart.
Also he durst not cough in case
he farted, which saved everyone
from a force 10.

The sound of lifts whizzing up
and down twenty storeys of his tubes
made him dizzy: a thousand
telephone bells pinging in his pores
got through to the inner ear
which, if disturbed, causes
loss of equilibrium and vomiting –
terrible thought.

To reduce nausea and save little lives
he turned his head sideways,
cleared his throat, (panic here)
and spat into the swimming-pool,
overflowing it. Obese guests
were washed out of the exercise-
lanes and swept away, crying:
this is giantism at its worst.

To the Lord of Rimini Met on Pewley Down

Suzerain of malarial sands, duke of artists and lagoons,
why d'you stroll these alien downs?
Perhaps to help me limp and stumble?
It should do so,
patron of the afterglow.
Malatesta, love my show.

By the homeward muddy track crows peck, violent in despair
at the flint grotesques turned up by the raping plough.
This is all their food today – stone on stone.
Cruel to ape a creature's bread.
Poet, cripple, hold your head.
Malatesta bakes your bread.

Here we're passing by a hollow last year painted blue in flowers
never to be harvested. Only images of power will flourish –
precious land for palaces – when this hill is sold.
Down the valley runs a train
like a disappearing pain.
Malatesta, are we sane?

So much music on the down – microlites fly overhead,
skylarks higher rise and rise, hanging out beyond their breath,
cursing at the twelve-shear plough as it buries all the blue.
At our picnic, kestrel's nouse
murders humble, crumbing mouse.
Malatesta, meet Lord Faust.

Be the patron of his sin, finance all his cunning pride,
listen to his corporate play on the theme of selling self
to the Satan deep inside. Watch your step over this stretch,
this is where the knee can wreck.
Damn your eyes, I'm on the deck.
Malatesta, break your neck.

Guildford, 2000

The Colours of Canaries

The trees are full of brown canaries.
Lilies with devil's parts lean out
of hedges. Passing thunder owes
tribute to the mountain. The singer
belts out her song to cool and quell
the melting of the earth. On this island,
the volcano is everything in life and art.

A geneticist from here, blinded by sulphur,
bred yellowness into the world's canaries,
wanting to share all he had left to see.
The volcano, quiet for three hundred years,
is overdue for an outburst of passionate
earthsong. When it does blow, the brown canaries
will be streaked with yellow as they sing
the song of the unchanged.

Mount Teide, Tenerife, 1986

To Santiago de Compostella with Shakespeare

Tragedies, comedies and histories
go into the rucksack with socks
and shirts, unlight reading
to be borne across Leon's plain,
through the desolation of Maragateria
over the Bierzo into the green maze
of Galicia. In his heart the hiker knows
the texts are there for ballast,
giving bottom to a pilgrim
not carrying the god.

Arriving at the shrine he sets down
his burden, embraces the altar statue
from behind, as is the custom,
puts his fingers, Saint Thomas-like,
into holes in the Gate of Glory (for luck),
makes a donation, receives written proof
of pilgrimage from the cardinal-archbishop's
secretary, puts the rucksack back over
his shoulder and prays
to Will for power.

Cabo Fisterra, 1982

Time for Meditation

Can't squeeze between these belfry girders
    so the cameras go up the tower without me,
    seeking a village panorama.
           Wait in a musty room,
           suspended half-way.

There's an old table, a chair thick with dust.
    Sweep them clean, then sit and listen
    to the ticking of the giant clock
           barely a yard away,
           caught by cliché.

Above, the photographers chatter and gaze,
    discerning design in human affairs – streets
    and gardens. Brood, brood,
           overclose to mechanism,
           hounded by minutes.

The hour cranks up. Gears rattle,
    groan and squeak. A vast bell booms
    right next the ear. Buzzing, shaken,
           hardly hear the others
           coming down the tower again.

Then, like a siren, my son is saying:
    I'll pick Dad up on my way down.
    Another knell, another chronic meaning.
           The boy is wrong – the way
           Down isn't his.

Later, the print is out, wet in the tray –
    the panorama from the tower –
    the sight I lost of mankind in the garden.
           But the gain is a week
           of tintinnabulums.

The Spanish Waiter

I have seen a hunchback here
each season for the last ten years,
waiting at my table with a smile
which doubled as a snarl.

Today, he comes
as customer, a young wife
on his arm, a baby sleeping
on his malformed shoulder.

He radiates contentment –
clearly loves his world.
His hair has silvered – it can
only be through happiness.

When he moves between the tables
care and courtesy from his old trade
are there, no snarl behind his smile
while serving past pain with joy.

Cool

Escaped to floor twenty-nine
to watch the Alberta dawn –
a prairie fire of light.
Dragons of headlamps hurry
into the city, red stopping-lights
bloodily spur the sides
of the sleeping day. Here oil
will go solid in the sump
if the car is left outside.
Without its motion, the sun
would freeze in this place.
Keep moving is the only motto.

On the roof, looking down on
the street-grid of Edmonton,
in the head-maze of heating exhausts,
in minus forty-three degrees,
there is someone tensed up and waiting
for a greater, gripping cold.
As the hotel sways in the Chinook wind.
he feels able to breathe landscapes
because this great block moves.
Certain days in life will be cold.
And certain days will demand
recourse to the swaying tower.

Held in Blue

Lost in low cloud, looking
        for a tarn to fish,
I followed the voice of a stream
        the map said had its source
in that water – the map you gave me
        of these mountain wastes.
Sticking to every twist
        and turn, I trudged along the bank,
knowing a wiser man would turn back,
        but I was not wise enough.
A rough wind came, tearing the cloud
        from the tops,
and I found myself in the tarn's empty bed,
        standing where the trout had swum.
But the map you gave me
        still held it in blue.
I folded it out in the wind,
        and thought deeply of you.

Limitations

We cannot change when we wish.
Growth and degeneration both are blessed
with alterations, not decisions.
Nature conspires against the good intentions
of her children – which is why the diet fails
and Falstaff dies a roaring tub, having taken
cream again for Shakespeare's sake.

Our sins are our adornment and our bridge
to better selves. Beneath the priestly nod
lurks the curse of fear. In the camera
at the wedding is mica fired in an inferno,
waiting for images of hell or happiness.
Nature obscures the light, bends down the corners of our books,
fills the smile of night with shame.

Limitations descend like chains when the head
is held most high, when the soul is bared
most brilliantly.

Who's Counting?

Well, cherub, your birthday
has come round again.

If you add up the two numbers
of your age it makes 9
which is the most important
digit in the creation

because after 9 we go back to 1
with a nought and start counting again
using all the existing numbers
reborn within what we know

also the numbers of 1998
when added together make 27,
and 2 and 7 make 9
which is amazing

Nostradamus has prophesied
that all those who have 9
in the climacteric of 9
will live to be 99 – one sees why

If we follow his maths
9 + 9 = 18 and 1 + 8 = 9
9 again, proving you are blessed
and amazing

It is heaping amazement upon amazement
to also record that your birthday
is the Feast of Saint Lucian of Antioch
who was drowned at sea

his body was brought to the beach
for burial by 9 dolphins
9 dolphins make a whale
amazing

M6

No road, no sign, no bridge
is visible from here. All I see
are the shapes of lorries shuttling though
our weeping ash. Parallelograms
roar north to Glasgow, cylinders
head south for London – geometry
in our green tree. Charmed by such power,
even the cat's whisker at the window
has a perfect curve –
the fielded bullock's neck is arched,
so Romanesque – the footprints of the feeding
birds are mystic triangles.
Before the great road came,
we were a mess, unclassical – bent at claw,
bowed at heel, odd at angle – now we rest lonely
on Euclid's hard shoulder.

Lancaster, 1977

Time of the Bindweed Flower

It was the time of the bindweed flower,
a beauty gardeners abhor –
white trumpets blazed from the hedge,
pale stamens pointing inwards to its powers
of conquest
that flourish when parental care
is low and trowels rust.

One blossom slipped into the house
by way of news left upon the phone –
smiling, as if he knew us well,
he put his feet up, opened the paper,
rewrote the headlines:
FATHER CLIMBS AWAY
between thorns on the rose-stem.

Turning to our half-finished crossword,
he changed every solved and unsolved clue,
reversed the lay-out, making all black,
white, all up, down – his way
of letting us know he intended to stay
for the rest of the daughter's life.

As he took his ease spreadeagled over
the heart of the house,
we looked askance at each other –
do something, say something,
comfort her, dig up that plunging root,
rip out those strangling vines,
keep weeds in check.
Garden tools left in the shed
have no power over the dead.

Vanishing Trick

Pleased at the news today.
Been worrying me lately, this issue –
Preying on my mind.
A strange surgical light
Sliced through my anxious gloom
This morning.
Now I feel much more comfortable
With the situation. Fear has abated
By about a third.
When I think of all the energy
I've put into this predicamental problem,
My brain goes into rinse and fast spin.
But the double millennia of high-powered
Intellectual product thrown in the bin today…wow!
The machine goes berserk.
      Should this shift of policy prove unpopular
And the e-mails start coming in saying:
How can we possibly live without Limbo?
It's so like contemporary life.
What then? Might the pope reverse the decision
And re-found it as an after-death colony
For dumbed-down souls?
Also, we must bear in mind that this construct –
Dismantled overnight like a motorway roadworks –
Is only one section of a giant complex
And the greater portion remains standing.
      As for the high-handed manner of the abolition itself –
here's a technical query:
It wasn't only unbaptized babies who were sent to Limbo.
Good heathens went there, and worthwhile pagans
Born before the coming of Christ
Who would have been Christians, given the chance.
Where have they all been transferred to?

Not back into life, and to Britain, one hopes.
We have enough problems.
    But never mind the small stuff. Let's talk big-time.
What about Purgatory? What about Hell?
Are they up for the chop as well?

October 2006

Julian

To be close to him was always to know the thorn before the rose
but you were sure the rose was there.
A resistance movement of his own,
ferocious critic of others and himself, in that order
(this would be torn to shreds – overwritten),
he was dissonance yearning for melody.
Words he adored more than notes, but wished they were the same.
He flowed, he ranted – goddamit, let's do it. Where is it?
What of it? You lost it? Then find it. Let's drink it
And talk it, dissect it, applaud it, abhor it, but anyway, have it.
Who's that woman you're with? Introduce me. What are you reading?
Don't bother – it's crap. Read this instead. A stylist supreme
with nothing to say. Knew him in Soho.

Here's what – we'll be quiet and listen to Schubert. He cheers me up so.
Hey, your breathing's too noisy. The asthmatic is me.

Hacksaw tongue. Feral eye. That stick of his.
Who was it underneath that hat?
A man employing wizardry on all folk but himself.
To pick his way carefully was heresy. Knew the wilderness
and all its fatalistic jokes.
Can't think of anyone I laughed with more, or had to rebuke more.
That laugh, that winding, demented cackle, sticks with you –
goosegrass on the mind.

Beethoven deliberately deafened himself
so he could hear better.
D'you follow? My, you're slow today. Sure I'll have another.
It'll keep me quiet while you work it all out.

Bedevilled of the Muse (and what a bitch she is),
you loved her too much to be able to please her.
To the hungry darkness every flame seems unquenchable
until it gutters in mid-proof and dies.
Fire is your dignity, Julian – fire.

Our Cat Hobbes

*For Christopher Smart and his cat Jeoffrey in Bethnal Green Asylum
in the 1760s and Jon and Carol and their cat Oliver in Slapton today.*

For I will consider our cat Hobbes
so you may know him and how he has a soul.

The tail of Hobbes is a marvel of length and significance.
It belongs to another world he is trying to reverse into
by means of his nether self.
His fur was left overnight in a tie-and-dye bucket
of blood and gold and his eyes are amber.
The harsh sound of his voice,
is stranger than the work of Stockhausen –
the only composer to ever give me a headache at a concert.
But these features do not single him out
as much as his fear of man-made danger.
Images of past and future peril
adhere like fridge magnets to the back of his mind.
All the bad things that can happen to a cat
lie in wait for Hobbes –
a pessimist down to his claw-ends.

The worst must come.
Brainless optimism is for the birds.

He sees me with my spade in the garden.
The amber eyes turn to red.
Are you digging that hole for me?
My wife and I are out walking a mile from home:
His eerie yowl comes from the hedge.
He has recognised our aimless chatter as we pass.
Why are you following me around?

At the roadside children are taught to look left then right
then left again before crossing if the way is clear.

Hobbes looks left then right then left then right then left then right
then turns round and goes back into the house.
Such is the paranoid nature of Hobbes.

The smell of catastrophe is always in his nostrils.
This is sad in a species that evolved into its present perfection
forty million years before the advent of Man.

When the perfected cat prowled across the continents
in the grace of complete evolutionary fulfilment,
Man was trying to decide whether to remain in the oceans
as a two-armed squid, be first cousin to the fruit-bat,
or start his remorseless career as super-predator
on all living things, including himself.

Man, the junior species, having taken aeons
to find direction, enchained the cat as substitute
for his own unevolved goodness.
When we stroke a cat, it is the best part of ourselves
that is under the hand.
We give cats house- and heart-room
as symbols of the selfhood beyond us.
If we had not domesticated the cat
our race would have destroyed itself long ago.

We got Hobbes from the forest rescue centre.
When we asked what he had been rescued *from*,
there was a tightening of the guardian's lip and a look
that said: *if you're a real cat lover, you won't want to know.*
In order to obtain him, we had to agree to neutering.
And pay in advance for the vet. That was the deal.

When we released him at home
he ran straight up the chimney.

When we had him neutered
his distrust was magnified an hundred times.
In the aftermath he wouldn't come near us,
spending hours on top of a cupboard,
eyes bright with hurt.
They abuse me then want a cuddle.
The conjunction of viciousness and sentimentality in the human mind!
Once they get bored with me it will be the needle.

For months after, he rejected all affection.
If we picked him up he went rigid.
He would only eat when we left the room.
Yet were we patient – even when he scorned our patience.

But after a year, he climbed up on my wife's lap
one evening as she sat reading by the fire,
parking himself across the open pages of her book
as if to say: never mind that, read this.

We held our breath, not daring to move.
Had we been accepted?
It was more important than being accepted
when we moved into the village.

Now, when he's in the mood, he brings his five kilogrammes
to the sofa: I'm here to tell you that I'm now one of the family.
Our mutual beasthood is everything to me.

We provide Hobbes with a home, food, admiration,
and obedience. He works hard to repay us.
Without doubt he is an ethical cat.
For our spiritual benefit he brings the environment
into our daily life:
the headless rat upon the Persian carpet –

the mole in the television room –
the rabbit ears under the kitchen table –
the greenfinch feathers in the bathroom.
When the piano-tuner comes
to repair a malfunctioning soft pedal,
the mummified head of a wood-pigeon
is found wedged under the mechanism.

Yes, Hobbes can lift lids and open doors
and he loves loud piano music,
but strings send him from the room in a huff
of insulted sensibilities.

He also has a limited power of speech
with which he chats and chunters.
Speak to him and he'll always answer,
often at length, sharing his meditations.
But one sharp sound…one false move…and he's off.
A long streak of hooped red, tail lashing as he disappears into the
undergrowth, the fear of man re-awakened.

But I conjecture that after five years with us
this fear has become more considered.
Though we are more likely to harm ourselves than he is,
I conjecture that he finds our addiction
to images of violence profoundly sad.
Who can trust a creature that delights in suffering
provided it isn't his?
Certainly, if Hobbes comes into the television room,
he always sits with his back to the screen.
I conjecture that he notes
how gorged we are with indigestible information.
I conjecture he thinks that, in spite of his efforts,
we remain an unnatural kind of animal.

I conjecture that he has found a way into
the book we have on how to keep cats.
He disputes all its assertions.
I conjecture that he is writing his own book
on how to keep humans
in which he says our instincts are flawed and twisted
by the preposterous predicament of having to earn money.

These could be the soul-altering thoughts of Hobbes
as he sits in private dignity by the fire,
his time-honoured, erect Egyptian dignity.
On the banks of the Nile he would have been a god,
but a god afraid of mankind because his worshippers trained him,
their cat-god, to guard granaries from mice,
starving and beating him when he failed.

So Hobbes keeps a watchful eye on adoration, veneration
and any form of ritualized behaviour on our part.
He looks upon all faiths with even-handed disfavour.
When the singing from the chapel next door
starts up on Sunday morning,
he goes off into the country to find a small hole somewhere.
He will sit outside this hole all day hoping to catch something.
That is his theology. Wait and see and pounce.
Humanity has never come near a religion worth having, he believes.
There is a cat-flap into the hereafter, but no man-flap.

Recently Hobbes and I contemplated each other.
I was in the conservatory, listening to the radio –
he was sitting very still on the lawn outside…in the pouring rain.
I waved to him, beckoning he should come in.
His lip lifted slightly in scorn,
then he curled up, tail over his eyes,
and slept in the downpour.

An hour later the rain stopped – only then did he move,
shaking away the worst the heavens could do.
I went out and looked where he'd slept.
The flattened grass was dry and warm,
an oval of separate green
where his soul had been.

A revelation had been granted me.
The mark of Hobbes was in his instinctual elsewhere,
the land where the soul lives free of pain.
Born in the forest he was taken from the wild,
not rescued from it.
His parents were not domesticated.
Someone had found him in the depths of the wood
and brought him out to save his soul from Paradise
by putting him in a cage.

No wonder he sleeps in the rain.
No wonder he thinks he's waterproof.
No wonder he lifts his head when the thunder rolls
but does not tremble.
The storm is the nearest he gets to a blessing.
The storm is the nearest he gets to his true power of life.
The storm is when he looks down upon us
from the height of his perfection.

Although we don't know why he stays,
we're glad he doesn't leave us.